EXPLORING
THE SUN

By Kate Rogers

KidHaven
PUBLISHING

Published in 2018 by
KidHaven Publishing, an Imprint of Greenhaven Publishing, LLC
353 3rd Avenue
Suite 255
New York, NY 10010

Designer: Deanna Paternostro
Editor: Vanessa Oswald

Photo credits: Cover Aphelleon/Shutterstock.com; back cover, p. 13 Vadim Sadovski/ Shutterstock.com; pp. 4–5 alexaldo/Shutterstock.com; p. 7 Amanda Carden/Shutterstock.com; p. 9 NASA images/Shutterstock.com; p. 11 cigdem/Shutterstock.com; p. 15 Mr. Yotsaran/ Shutterstock.com; p. 17 Ivannn/Shutterstock.com; p. 19 solarseven/Shutterstock.com; p. 21 Todoranko/Shutterstock.com.

Cataloging-in-Publication Data

Names: Rogers, Kate.
Title: Exploring the sun / Kate Rogers.
Description: New York : KidHaven Publishing, 2018. | Series: Journey through our solar system | Includes index.
Identifiers: ISBN 9781534522923 (pbk.) | 9781534522787 (library bound) | ISBN 9781534522503 (6 pack) | ISBN 9781534522664 (ebook)
Subjects: LCSH: Sun–Juvenile literature.
Classification: LCC QB521.5 R635 2018 | DDC 523.7–dc23
Printed in the United States of America

CPSIA compliance information: Batch #BS17KL: For further information contact Greenhaven Publishing LLC, New York, New York at 1-844-317-7404.

Please visit our website, www.greenhavenpublishing.com. For a free color catalog of all our high-quality books, call toll free 1-844-317-7404 or fax 1-844-317-7405.

CONTENTS

The sun is the only star in our **solar system**.

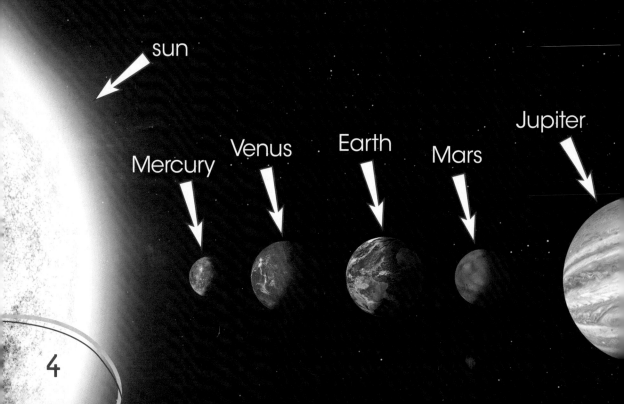

sun

Mercury Venus Earth Mars Jupiter

The sun is about 4.6 billion years old!

All eight planets **orbit** around the sun in a part of space known as the Milky Way **galaxy**.

Saturn

Uranus

Neptune

The sun could fit about 1 million Earths inside of it. This star contains most of the matter in our solar system. This makes it one of the largest objects we know of in space.

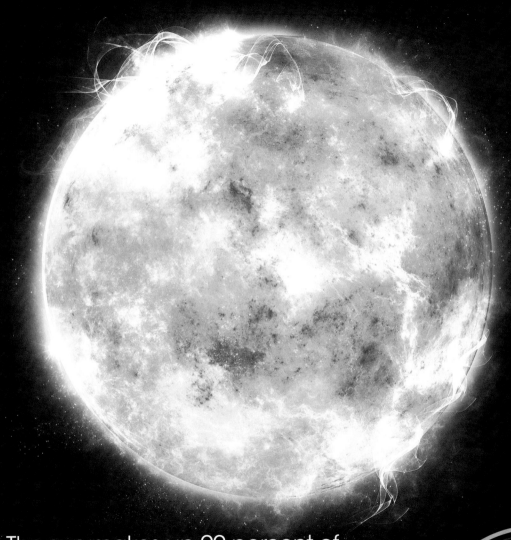

The sun makes up 99 percent of
all of the mass in our solar system.

FULL OF GASES

The sun is mostly made up of **hydrogen** and **helium**. These gases are two of the most common gases in the solar system. All stars are made up of a **mixture** of gases.

The sun is a yellow dwarf star. Dwarf stars are stars as big as or smaller than the sun. Giant stars are bigger than the sun and are outside of our solar system.

Gravity causes the sun's gases to form into a tight, hot ball. This changes the star's hydrogen into helium. The sun's gravity also keeps planets and other smaller objects in space in orbit around it.

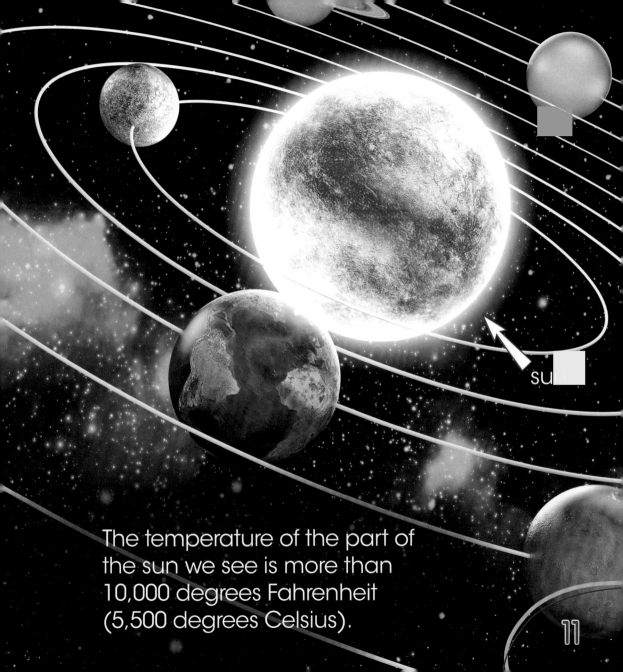

sun

The temperature of the part of the sun we see is more than 10,000 degrees Fahrenheit (5,500 degrees Celsius).

THE SUN'S ENERGY

The sun gives a large amount of heat and light to Earth. It's our most powerful source of **energy**. People wouldn't be able to live on Earth without the sun.

It takes more than eight minutes for light from the sun to reach Earth.

The sun helps create our planet's seasons, weather, and **climate**. The sun also creates weather in the solar system with **solar wind**.

The energy from the
sun also helps create
Earth's ocean currents.

THE SURFACE OF THE SUN

Sometimes dark, cooler areas can be seen on the sun's surface. Scientists have named these areas sunspots. A single sunspot can be bigger than Earth!

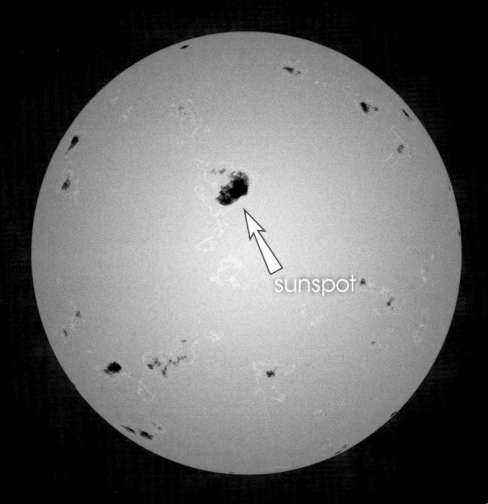

sunspot

The first sunspots were viewed
through a **telescope** in 1610.

Explosions called solar flares will sometimes burst from the sun's surface. These blasts can cause giant flames to shoot into space. Solar flares also cause power outages on Earth.

The first solar flare
was discovered on
September 1, 1859.

19

A CHANGING SUN

In billions of years, the sun will grow bigger and hotter. Its yellow color will change to red. After this, the sun will grow smaller and cooler. Luckily, this won't happen in our lifetime!